CREMATION: CHRISTIAN OR PAGAN?

By

Dennis D. Helton

DEDICATION

Dedicated to faithful Christian women who have stood in the gap so many, many times.

Dennis D. Helton
February 2021

TABLE OF CONTENTS

CREMATION: CHRISTIAN OR PAGAN?

Cremation process

Cremation itself is the process of reducing the body remains to bone fragments and ashes through burning with open flames. The temperature of 1,600-2000 degrees Fahrenheit is maintained for approximately two to three hours (note: tin melts at 450 deg. F; lead melts at 662 deg. F). The ashes of a body's cremation are usually mingled with the ashes of a body of a previous cremation. The larger bones remaining are usually ground up to smaller pieces.

The writer's opinion

Today, even Christians are exploring cremation as an option to burial. The writer does not believe that cremation is acceptable for the Christian. Cremation has always been practiced by pagans and adherents of false religions. For example, the Hindus and Buddhists do not believe in a resurrection of the body; they believe that their soul is reincarnated (transmigrated) into another unrelated body or even a non-physical existence. By burning the bodies of the dead, they superstitiously hoped to prevent that body's spirit from remaining in the local area and haunting the living. Of course, as Christians, we know death is the separation of the soul and spirit from the dead body.

Jeremiah 10:2: Thus saith the LORD, Learn not the way of the heathen.

Origin of the practice of cremation

The *Encyclopedia Britannica* reported,

"The Scandinavians favored cremation, believing that it helped free the spirit from the flesh and also that it kept the dead from harming the living. These pagan practices paralleled the Greek and Roman epic cremations." *(Encyclopedia Britannica,* 15th Edition, p. 726).

The Encarta Encyclopedia 2005 says,

"Evidence of cremation dates from antiquity; ashes of several individuals have been found throughout Europe. Between 1400 BC and AD 200, cremation was the preferred burial custom, especially among Roman aristocrats."

Between the 3rd and 19th century, anemic Christianity forbade cremation because of the belief that the body could not be resurrected if it were destroyed. Early Jews also prohibited cremation, believing it was the desecration of a work of God. Orthodox Jews, the Eastern Orthodox churches, and Muslims are still forbidden to cremate their dead. Other groups of people, especially in India, continued to practice cremation and still do today. Today, cremation is practiced by some Jews and Christians. It is also practiced by Buddhists, Sikhs, and Hindus.

Beginning of English speaking people to practice cremation

A society advocating cremation was founded in England in 1874. The first crematorium in the United States was established in Washington, Pennsylvania, in 1876.

Initially, there was opposition to cremation out of the fear that forensic evidence of murder might be destroyed.

Today there are memorial gardens and buildings called *columbaria* with niches where ash-filled urns can be stored and visited by relatives. Cremation has rapidly increased in the United States from 8.5 percent of deaths in 1978 to 15.3 percent of deaths in 1988.

Why cremation has gained acceptance

There are three principal reasons that cremation has gained such popularity (other than the civilized becoming tainted with paganism):

a) **economics**

b) **sanitary (health) considerations**

c) **lack of and cost of burial space**

a) Economics: Explosive population growth has lessened space for burial plots and land has become scarce and expensive. Adding to the already high cost of the burial plot is the vault, casket, marker, opening of the ground, perpetual care, and the mortuary expense of about $6,000.00 (at the time of this writing in Greenville, SC).

b) Sanitary Considerations: In-ground burial can **contaminate** water supplies for entire communities. It is especially serious when death has been caused by a highly contagious disease and threatens to contaminate underground water tables. At one time, arsenic was part of the embalming process. Caskets and corpses have risen from in-ground burial to above ground many times during severe flooding,

However, you cannot separate cremation from *paganism* and *heathenism*. Cremation (burning) has a close affinity to **Hell fire** (Matthew 13:50; 18:8, 9; Mark 9:43, 44, 45, 46, 47, 48)!

c) Lack of burial space: According to Mike Gipson at the Tidewater Cemetery Corporation of Virginian Beach, Virginia, "a thousand people can be buried in one acre of land." He also indicted that, "in some of the local cemeteries there are two bodies in some graves." Of course, the limiting factor for many low income people without sufficient insurance coverage is the cost of the burial plots themselves.

Cremation statistics

In the United States (presently 2,000 AD), with over 22,000 Funeral Homes:

• 28 cremations were recorded between 1876-1884

• by 1977, 7 % of all bodies were cremated

• by 1993, nearly 20 % of all bodies were cremated

- Presently (2001), 25 % of all bodies are cremated

"Ashes to ashes" is not of the Bible

Although the Bible does teach that the body will return to dust, it does not teach "*ashes to ashes*".

> *Genesis 3:19: In the sweat of thy face shalt thou eat bread, till thou return unto the **ground**; for out of it wast thou taken: for dust thou art, and **unto dust shalt thou return**.*

It is not "cinders and ashes to cinders and ashes" but "dust to dust." In many of the usages of the word "ashes" in Scriptures, a repenting, humility, or the humbling of man to a low estate is meant. In other passages, the "burning of sacrifices to ashes" pictures judgment of sin, not the burial of the body.

Who owns the body?

> *I Corinthians 6:19-20: What Know ye not that **your body is the temple of the Holy** Ghost which is in you, which ye have of God, and **ye are not your own**? For ye are bought with a price: therefore **glorify God in your body**, and in your spirit, which are God's.*

To this writer, a burning (cremation) of the body does not glorify God. The writer wonders if the families of the deceased (who can well afford the expense of a proper burial) even consult with God over the matter of cremation.

Cremation not practiced in the Bible

Some would approve of cremation of the body based upon the single isolated instance of the burning of Saul and his son's bodies (I Samuel 31:12). They would boldly assert that this was Bible justification for cremation of the body?

> *I Samuel 31:9-13: And they (Philistines) cut off his (Saul's) head, and stripped off his armour, and sent into the land of the Philistines round about, to publish it in the house of their idols, and among the people. And they put his armour in the house of Ashtaroth: and they fastened his body to the wall of Beth-shan. And when the inhabitants of Jabesh-gilead heard of that which the Philistines had done to Saul; All the valiant men arose, and went all night, and took the body of Saul and the bodies of his sons from the wall of Beth-shan, and came to Jabesh, and **burnt them** there. And they took their bones, and **buried** them under a tree at Jabesh, and fasted seven days.*

The Philistines had:

- Cut off Saul's head and fastened (or, hung) it to the temple of Dagon (I Chronicles 10:10)
- Stripped Saul's armour and displayed it in their pagan temple (I Chronicles 10:10)
- Fastened (or hung) Saul and his son's bodies to the wall of Beth-shan (I Samuel 31:12)

10

- Published these things all through the land of the Philistines and round about (I Samuel 31:9)

Under OT law, the highest degree of disgrace and reproach was the public **hanging** of the body. He that is **hanged** is accursed of God (Deuteronomy 21:23; Acts 5:30; 10:39). To hang between heaven and earth concludes the victim abandoned of both heaven and earth and unworthy of either.

(**Hanged:** The biblical hangings were not by the neck unto death as are modern day hangings.)

NOTE: Christ redeemed us from the curse of the law (accursed of God) by being Himself made a curse for us (Galatians 3:13). The law was satisfied and our guilt removed when we received Jesus' propitiation for our sins (I John 2:1-4).

The meaning of the burning the bodies may be one of three possibilities: a) the burning of incense for the body as was done usually for kings, b) to purify from disease, c) to prevent further desecration by the Philistines. The well-meaning men of Jabesh properly **buried their bones** under a tree. Notice that the proper **burial** of Saul and Jonathan's bones was highly blessed by King David (II Samuel 2:4-5; 21:12-14). Observe that the burning of these bodies was **the choice of the men**. The burning of the bodies was **not ordered by God** any more than the action of Saul was ordered of God when he demanded that his armourbearer thrust him through with his sword. It is likely that the bodies of this royal family (which were mutilated, bird-picked, and decaying) were burned with spices and sweet odors

11

to honor them and to prevent further desecration of them by the Philistines and also to halt the shame that was being heaped upon Israel ("Tell it not in Gath" - I Samuel 27:11; 2 Samuel 1:20). Some think that the putrefying flesh was sweetened by burning. Others think that ointments were burned on their flesh for a proper burial. Regardless of the burning, it was not ordered by God.

Second Chronicles 16 speaks of the **burning of spices** at the funeral of a king in honor for the good things that he had done and in respect for his royalty.

> *2 Chronicles 16:14: And they **buried him** (King Asa) in his own sepulchers, which he had made for himself in the city of David, and laid him in the bed which was filled with **sweet odours** and **divers kinds of spices** prepared by the apothecaries art: and they **made a very great burning** for him.*

God was displeased with Moab for **burning** (cremating) the **bones** of the king of Edom and sent a judgment of fire (Amos 2:1). Fire is used many times in the Bible as a sign of God's curse and judgment upon sin.

A public cremation observed

According to the April-June *Circuit Rider*, p. 6, David Cloud witnessed a public cremation. "I stood three or so feet from a burning corpse with a missionary pastor in Singapore and his wife who were visiting us. The head was already burnt beyond recognition and the skull was split open due to internal expansion from the heat of the fire. The lower legs and feet were unscorched, as they were protruding from the pile of burning wood and stubble upon which the man's body lay. The professional Hindu burners were poking the body from time to time to keep the members in the fire and adding stubble and wood as needed. The bones were contracting and popping: the bodily organs were frying and the juices sizzling in the intense heat...The air for a hundred yards or more was filled with the unmistakable, stomach-turning stench of burning human flesh (The writer has experienced this unforgettable smell after helping a mortician carry a burned body of a dead man after a car wreck in Plant City, FL).

Fire or burning (cremation) often speaks of judgment:

- God destroyed Sodom and Gomorrah with **fire** (Genesis 19:24)

- God used **fire** to judge Nadab and Abihu for their inappropriate sacrifices (Leviticus 10:1-2)

- God used **fire** to punish those who were insubordinate to the spiritual leadership of Moses(Numbers 16:1-32, 35)

- Disobedient Achan was stoned and burned with **fire** (John 7:15, 25)

- God's final judgment of this world will be by **fire** (2 Peter. 3:12)

- The final habitation for those who reject Christ will be in a place of **fire** (Hell -Mark 9; **the lake of fire** - Revelation 20:15).

Today (2,000 A.D.) in Christendom, many mortuaries are offering crematorium service. One mortuary says that cremation accounts for 50% of "their" final dispositions.

How should Christians handle the dead body if cremation is not an option?

God instructed Israel to **bury** a sinner that was worthy of death the very day that he was hung upon a tree rather than allowing the sinner's body to hang upon the tree all night

> *Deuteronomy 21:23: His body shall not remain all night upon the tree, but thou shalt in any wise **bury** him that day; (for he that is hanged is accursed of God;) that thy land be not defiled, which the LORD thy God giveth thee for an inheritance.*

Burial was consistent with OT Jewish history, NT Christianity, and the early church:

- God practiced **burial** with **Moses** (Deuteronomy 34:5-6; Jude 9).

- God's people have always practiced **burial.** Note the following:

-Abraham - Gen. 25:8-10

-Sarah - Gen. 23:1-4

-Deborah - Gen. 35:8-9

-Isaac - Gen. 35:27-29

-Jacob - Gen. 50:1-13

-**Rachel** - Gen. 35:19-20

-**Joseph** - Gen. 50:26

-**Miriam** - Num. 20:1

-**Aaron** - Num. 20:23-29

-**Joshua** - Josh. 24:29-30

-**Eleazar** - Josh. 24:33

-**Samuel** - I Sam. 25:1

-**David** - I Kings 2:10

-**Lazarus** - John 11:1-46

-**Samson** - Jdg. 16:31

-The **widow of Zarephath's son** - I Kings 17:17-24

-**Stephen** - Acts 8:2

-The **Shunammittes's son** - II Kings 4:18-37

-**John the Baptist** - Matt. 14:10-12

-**Ananias** and **Sapphira** -- Acts 5:6, 10

-**JESUS CHRIST** Himself received a proper burial in a borrowed tomb (**Luke** 23:52-53)

Cremation vs. the figure of Christian baptism

Cremation of Christians does away with the full meaning of the ordinance of "water baptism" by denying a **burial** of the body (burial of ashes or scattering of them on land or water can hardly be construed as the burial of the body.

*Romans 6:4: Therefore we are **buried*** [figurately] *with him by water baptism] into* *death: that like as Christ was raised up from the dead by the glory of the Father, even so we also should walk in newness of life.*

Burning or cremation does not simulate or symbolize a burial and resurrection of the body, as does water baptism.

*Colossians 2:12: **Buried** with him in baptism, wherein also ye are risen with him through the faith of the operation of God, who hath raised him from the dead.*

*I Peter 3:21: **The like figure** whereunto **even baptism** doth also now save us (not the putting away of the filth of the flesh, but the answer of a good conscience toward God) by the resurrection of Jesus Christ.*

Baptism is a figure of *burial*, not burning or cremation. Of course, "water baptism" is a figure of *salvation*. Baptism is a picture of **death** to the old man, **burial** (simulated in baptismal waters), and **resurrection** to newness of life (coming up out of the baptismal waters).

The baptism of the Holy Spirit is pictured by "water baptism." The Holy Spirit baptizes us into the body of Christ:

*I Corinthians 12:13: For **by one Spirit are we all baptized into one body**, whether we be Jews or Gentiles, whether we be bond or free; and have been all made to drink into one Spirit.*

There is only one "Spirit baptism:"

Ephesians 4:4-6: There is one body, and one Spirit, even as ye are called in one

16

*hope of your calling; One Lord, one faith, **one baptism**, One God and Father of all, who is above all, and through all, and in you all.*

Man is a tripartite being of body, soul, and spirit (I Thessalonians 5:23) and originally created in God's image (Genesis 1:27). That image now has been marred by sin. All parts belong to God. A person that is born again (John 3:3, 5, 7) is God's temple. Although the soul and spirit is no longer in its tabernacle of flesh [the dead body], cremation still dishonors the former temple of the soul.

*I Corinthians 6:19-20: What? know ye not that **your body is the temple of the Holy Ghost** which is in you, which ye have of God, and ye are not your own? For ye are bought with a price: therefore glorify God in your body, and in your spirit, which are God's.*

Cost of burial versus the cost of cremation

The writer is aware that some choose cremation instead of burial because of their economic situation. The minimum cost of cremation begins at about $1,800 (Greenville, SC, March 2002) while the minimum cost today for a funeral and burial is about $10,000. Without adequate insurance, this is a prohibitive expense to many that are struggling day-to-day to get by on a small income. Only those responsible for the burial can make the right choice.

The writer does not sit in judgment of those who cremate their loved ones out of the necessity of poverty.

Does Cremation affect the believer's life after death?

The improper handling of the dead body (cremation; burning; mutilation; etc.) will not, in any way, affect the person's soul or his resurrection body. Proper burial of the dead body is a show of respect to the deceased and honors our Creator, who is the Giver of life. We should have a high regard for the dead body, not to enshrine and adore it as relics are commonly worshipped, but to carefully deposit the body in **burial**. The dead body of the *believer* is designed for glory and immortality at the last day. Though the body be accidentally burned or intentionally cremated, God is sovereign and has power over ashes, dust, and atoms. It will be no problem for God to re-assemble the atoms in the day of resurrection when believers will receive a glorified body.

(Relics: Viz., tooth of Buddha; Big toe of Peter's statue; shroud of Turin; et al.)

A Christian friend that wants to be cremated

A professing Christian friend remarked to this writer that upon death he wanted to be cremated rather than buried. When I asked him why, he said that he could not bear the thought of being buried under the cold ground (as if he thought the soul and spirit of man remained in the body). Fully aware that the soul and spirit of man did not remain in the dead body and knowing that my friend was claustrophobic, I reminded him that it was a far more fearful thing to be placed into a red-hot furnace heated up to 2,000 degrees Fahrenheit than under the cold earth (many metals melt below 2,000 degrees Fahrenheit).

For the believer, to be absent from the body (death) is to be present with the Lord (2 Corinthians 5:8). Again, death is the separation of the spirit and soul from the body. The body in the grave is an empty shell (without a soul and spirit).

The unbeliever, rich or poor, will not be with Christ upon death; he will open his eyes in Hell (Luke 16:22-23).

Again, when the souls of the deceased depart from the dead body, there are only two places or eternal habitats for them, **Heaven** or **Hell** (Matthew 7:13, 14; 25:41, 46; Mark 9:43-48; Luke 16:19-31; John 14:3; 2 Corinthians 5:2; Philippians 3:10; Colossians 1:5;

I Thessalonians 1:10; 4:16; I Peter 1:4; Revelation 20:6, 11-15). The only person in the universe that can determine their everlasting habitat is that person himself.

Jesus said to unbelievers

John 5:40: And ye will not come to me, that ye might have life.

-It is not that the sinner "cannot" come but that he "will not" come to Christ.

John 8:24: I said therefore unto you, that ye shall die in your sins: for if ye believe not that I am He (Saviour of the world; promised Messiah), ye (all unbelievers) shall die in your sins.

Everyone will be resurrected

Everyone, from Adam to the last person, will come forth from the dead (in his order) in a literal resurrection body.

> John 5:28-29: Marvel not at this; for the hour is coming, in the which **all** that are in the graves (spirits and souls of both saved and lost men reunited with their bodies) *shall hear his voice, And shall come forth; they that have done good, unto the **resurrection of life**; and they that have done evil, unto the **resurrection of damnation**.*

The two major resurrections of the saved and the unsaved are one-thousand years apart:

> Revelation 20:5-6: But the rest of the dead lived not again until the **thousand years** were finished. This is the first resurrection. Blessed and holy is he that hath part in the first resurrection: on such the second death hath no power, but they shall be priests of God and of Christ, and shall reign with him a thousand years.

(Note: the two major resurrections are either one-thousand or one-thousand and seven years apart (determined by which end of the Tribulation Period [Daniel's 70th Week of Prophecy] that you count from.)

Again, there will be two major (but separate) judgments:

1.) Believers: All believers will have part in the First Resurrection (Revelation 20:6) and will appear at the **Judgment Seat of Christ** to answer for their stewardship, faithfulness, and reception or loss of rewards (not sins) - Romans 14:10; II Corinthians 5:10: I Corinthians 3:12-15).

*II Corinthians 5:10: For we (believers in Christ) must all appear before **the judgment seat of Christ**; that every one may receive the things done in his body, according to that he hath done, whether if be good or bad.*

Jesus said unto the repentant thief on the cross, **Verily I say unto thee, Today shalt thou be with me in Paradise** (Luke 23:43). **Paradise** was called *Abraham's bosom* by the Jews and was the place believers were carried to by angels (Luke 16:22; 23:43). The Paradise section of Sheol (or Hades) is the part where Jesus probably went to between His death and resurrection or shortly thereafter (Ephesians 4:9; Matthew 27:51-54).

Paradise was moved to Heaven (Ephesians 4:8-10; 2 Corinthians 12:2-4).

2.) Unbelievers: All of the unsaved dead will be resurrected and shall stand before God at the **Great White Throne.** They will be judged for their sin according to their works, and then death and Hell, and they shall be cast into the lake of fire (Revelation 20:5-6, 11-15).

There is no "purgatory," "limbo state," "middle ground" or "second chance" after death as taught by false religions. Upon death, the eternal habitat is forever established either in Heaven or Hell.

> *Acts 24:15: "...that there shall be **a resurrection** of the dead, **both of the just and unjust.**"*

> *Revelation 20:11-15: And I saw **a great white throne**, and him that sat on it, from whose face the earth and heaven fled away; and there was found no place for them. And I saw the **dead** (unsaved: lost), small and great, stand before God; and the books were opened: and another book was opened which is the book of life, and the **dead** (unsaved) were judged out of those things which were written in the books according to their works...*

> *And the sea gave up the dead which were in it; and death and Hell delivered up the dead which were in them; and they were judged every man according to their works. And death and Hell were cast into the **lake of fire**. This is the **second death**. And whosoever was not found written in the book of life was cast into the **lake of fire**.*

Tophet (Hell) is the residence for unbelievers. The Hell section of Sheol was a place of sorrows (2 Samuel 22:6; Psalms 18:5; 116:3; Luke 16:23). The unsaved wicked are turned into this place (Psalms 9:17).

Hell itself, a place of **flames** and torments (Luke 16:23, 24), is itself cast into the **lake of fire,** which is the second death (Revelation 20:14)

Upon death, man will be without excuse before God

Salvation is NOT a hard thing to understand; salvation is made plain and simple.

> *Acts 16:30-31: "…Sirs, what must I do to be saved? And they said, **Believe on the Lord Jesus Christ**, and thou shalt be saved, and thy house.*

> *Ephesians 2:8-9: For by grace are ye saved through faith; and that not of yourselves: it is **the gift of God**: Not of works, lest any man should boast.*

Pride, rebellion, and procrastination (neglect; putting off until another day) are three great enemies of the soul.

> *Hebrews 2:2-3: For if the word spoken by angels was stedfast, and every transgression and disobedience received a just recompence of reward; How shall we escape, if we **neglect** so great salvation; which at the first began to be spoke by the Lord, and was confirmed unto us by them that heard him.*

If someone rushed into a man's house urging him to get out immediately because the house was on fire and may collapse, would a sensible man believe him and escape the fire? If the inhabitant had good sense, he would exit the house immediately. Certainly, a rational person that really believed in Hell would heed the warning of God's Word. Yet, multitudes will not believe the Word of God when his faithful children try to warn them to flee to God and escape the fire and torment of Hell.

God's warnings are far more certain than any warning by man of a burning house!

The punishment of Hell is so horrible that Christ Himself warns us to literally eliminate any body parts that would hinder our escape from that place of torment. Of the twelve times that Gehenna (hell-fire) is used in the New Testament, eleven of those were by Jesus Christ Himself (once by James).

Hell is no joke (Mark chapter 9:43-48)

*Verse 43: And if **thy hand** offend thee, cut it off: it is better for thee to enter into life maimed, than having two hands to go into hell, into **the fire** that never shall be quenched:*

*Verse 44: Where their worm dieth not, and **the fire** is not quenched.*

*Verse 45: And if **thy foot** offend thee, cut it off: it is better for thee to enter halt into life, than having two feet to be cast into hell, into **the fire** that never shall be quenched:*

*Verse 46: Where their worm dieth not, and **the fire** is not quenched.*

*Verse 47: And if **thine eye** offend thee, pluck it out: it is better for thee to enter into the kingdom of God with one eye, than having two eyes to be cast into **hell fire**:*

*Verse 48: Where their worm dieth not, and **the fire** is not quenched.*

Luke 16:23-24: "And in Hell he lift up his eyes, being in torments...for I am tormented in this flame."

Many unbelievers make sport of being consigned to Hell and insanely state that they will be with their buddies and have a good time partying. Even upon earth, it would be difficult to fellowship with anyone while in great pain and torment; how much more difficult would partying and fellowship if in the fire of Hell? The writer even doubts that you will be able to locate your buddies in the darkness of the thick flames.

The story is told of an atheist who took pleasure in constantly haranguing a young, simple-minded, and unlearned boy concerning the boy's faith in God. The young man posed a solemn scenario to the atheist: He told the atheist that if he himself was wrong about the bliss of Heaven and the judgment of Hell and they both died, neither had lost anything; however, if he was correct about Heaven and Hell, he had gained his soul and everlasting joy, but the atheist had forever lost his soul in anguish of Hell fire forever.

For the sinner, **Death is the king of terror**.

How to go to Heaven

In order to go to Heaven and escape the fire of Hell, Jesus told a religious man (Nicodemus, a Pharisee – John 3:1-16) that a man must be **born again** (Viz., not be baptized; join a church; pay your dues; do your best; et al). Of course, Jesus was speaking of being born again by the Spirit of God

(John 3:3, 5, 7; I Corinthians 12:13; Romans 8:9). Many Baptists, Methodists, Presbyterians, Catholics, Lutherans, Pentecostals, Charismatics, and Episcopalians will go to Hell trusting only in a religious experience or an ordinance instead of repentance and faith for salvation. Of course, this applies to any others of any sectarian religion that is depending upon good works outweighing bad works, ordinances, or anything else to save them. Hell will be filled with unsaved people who were church members. Everyone has a religion. Christ is not a religion. What this writer or anyone else say has no meaning whatsoever unless it is true to Scripture.

Luke 13:3: I tell you, Nay: but, except ye repent, ye shall all likewise perish.

Acts 16:30-31: And brought them out, and said, Sirs, what must I do to be saved? And they said, Believe on the Lord Jesus Christ, and thou salt be saved, and thy house.

Ephesians 2:8-9: For by grace are ye saved through faith: and that not of yourselves: it is the gift of God: Not of works, lest any man should boast.

Romans 10:9-10, 13, 17: That if thou shalt confess with thy mouth the Lord Jesus, and shalt believe in thine heart that God hath raised him from the dead, thou shalt be saved. For with the heart man believeth unto righteousness; and with the mouth confession is made unto salvation. For whosoever shall call upon the name of the Lord shall be saved. So then faith cometh by hearing, and hearing by the word of God

ABOUT THE AUTHOR

The writer was born in Greenville, SC in 1934 and was a lifetime resident with the exception of two years in the US Army (Fort Jackson, S.C. and Fort Carson, Colorado) and two years residence in Florida.

After separation (honorably) from the US Army, the writer returned to Greenville, SC and married at age 27 to Christine Moore, an old acquaintance from an adjacent neighborhood. The Lord blessed us with six daughters, Debbie, Donna, Dale, Denise, Deree, and Dena.

A short time after marriage, the writer was convicted of his lost condition as a sinner and after a miserable time under conviction the writer confessed his sin and lost condition to God and was saved.

The writer was 40 years of age when he began attending college (3 years, no diploma).

The writer retired as a chemical technologist from Morton International Chemical Company in 1996. Before retirement, the writer had the urge to write on Bible subjects and wished that he had more time to study. Upon retirement, the writer bought a computer and became a novice writer.

The writer now resides in Easley, S.C.

D. Helton has written several documents as well as the book, "Jesus is God" available here: http://www.theoldpathspublications.com/Pages/Auth ors/Helton.htm#God

www.ingramcontent.com/pod-product-compliance
Lightning Source LLC
Chambersburg PA
CBHW051052030426
42339CB00006B/311